IT'S TIME TO LEAVE THE
Cemetery

REPOSITIONING YOUR LIFE FOR THE NEXT BIG THING!

RAY BEVAN

All correspondence to:
Ray Bevan
The King's Church, 69 Lower Dock Street, Newport, Wales, NP20 1EH
Tel:+44(0)1633 244453
ray.bevan@kings-church.org.uk
www.kings-church.org.uk

Published by Integrity Media Europe
Unit 1 Hargreaves Business Park
Hargreaves Road, Eastbourne, BN23 6QW

ISBN 978-1-907080-02-9

IT'S TIME TO LEAVE THE Cemetery

REPOSITIONING YOUR LIFE FOR THE NEXT BIG THING!

RAY BEVAN

It's time to walk away from the cemetery and let God fulfil His will and His purposes concerning you!

PREFACE

Have you ever heard of the Kodiak bear? I hadn't until I'd watched a documentary about a mother and her cub and what happened when disaster struck. Early on in the filming the mother was killed and the cub was left all alone to fend for itself. With no experience in the art of survival, the cub spent its first five days never leaving the body of its dead mother. Finally in a quest to live it had to leave the lifeless corpse and find new sources of life and energy.

The same applies to all of us. Sometimes the things we trust in and the sources of strength that we rely upon begin to die, yet we find ourselves forever clinging to the past in a vain effort to survive. Like the young Kodiak bear, there comes a time to leave what was and search for new places to live and prosper. It's time to leave the cemetery. It's scary and heart-breaking, yet necessary for us to finish our course and fulfill our destiny.

This book is designed to help you do just that as well as bring closure to many of the yesterdays of our lives. It's time to say goodbye to past relationships, past hurts, old seasons and broken dreams. Lay your last flower at the grave and allow the words of this book to take you out of your cemetery and never look back. Your future awaits.

Ray Bevan

INTRODUCTION

All of my teenage years, I had a dream of becoming a rock star! It all started to go wrong when my band 'Robbie Ray and the Jaguars' decided to split! It was a sad day for three or four diehard fans, but an even sadder day for me – my dream of making it big was beginning to fall apart and my new life of working in a paint store certainly didn't offer me anything to hang my hopes on!

Three months after the band was well and truly dead, I tried to reform it. No one was interested, so I put all of my efforts into forming another band. In the midst of all of my striving to create a future for myself it was the words to one of the songs on our playlist that really spoke to me. I was busy singing Jamie Taylor's 'Fire and Rain' when I became aware of the words that I was singing.

'Won't you look down on me, Jesus
You've got to help me make a stand
You've just got to see me through another day
My body's aching and my time is at hand
and I won't make it any other way'

... 'oh, I've seen fire and I've seen rain ...'

This was the catalyst that I needed to help me let go of all of my best laid plans and turn to the God of destiny. Amongst His 'designer label' plans for me were things that were beyond anything that I could have ever imagined.

Secretly, I would have loved to have 'made it big', but if I had, I would have missed out on the greatest opportunity of all – to fulfil God's plan and purpose for my life.

As I look back, the collapse of 'Robbie Ray and the Jaguars' was one of the best things that has happened to me. It led me to the greatest decision of my life – to surrender my life completely into the hands of Jesus and to reposition myself for the next big thing ... and this was to be God's thing in my life.

It may be that everything around you is falling quicker than you can rebuild it. Maybe you've been pushing ahead with plans for marriage, business, career, friendships or simply something very close to your heart. To see it collapsing before you can be the hardest thing to ever deal with. Your future, however, could be depending on the very thing that is currently taking place. It could be that God is 'clearing the way' for His plans and purpose to arise. It may be that God is about to gazump you with stuff that you have never ever dreamed of.

The Bible even states that,

> *"No eye has seen no ear has heard no mind has conceived what God has prepared for those who love Him." (1 Corinthians 2:9)*

This book is about that very thing – the necessity for things to die in order that better things can live!

The greatest challenge in life is to accept the fact that some things have had their day. To prolong the agony of trying to keep things that have died alive is to hinder the onset of brand new things that God is waiting anxiously to give to you.

After the death and burial of Jesus, the Angels said to Mary Magdalene and Mary the mother of Jesus, 'Why do you look for the living amongst the dead?' (Luke 24:5) They were looking for Christ who was no longer there. They needed to leave the cemetery and live in the new season of the 'risen Christ'. This could be your time too to leave behind the cemetery of all that's past, broken, old and dead and head on up to higher ground.

The next big thing awaits and it's filled with all things new, fresh, alive and whole! It's time to go!

Past Relationships
Broken Dreams
Past Methods
Old Seasons
Past Hurts

CONTENTS

Past Relationships

Broken Dreams

Past Methods

Old Seasons

Past Hurts

1. Past Relationships

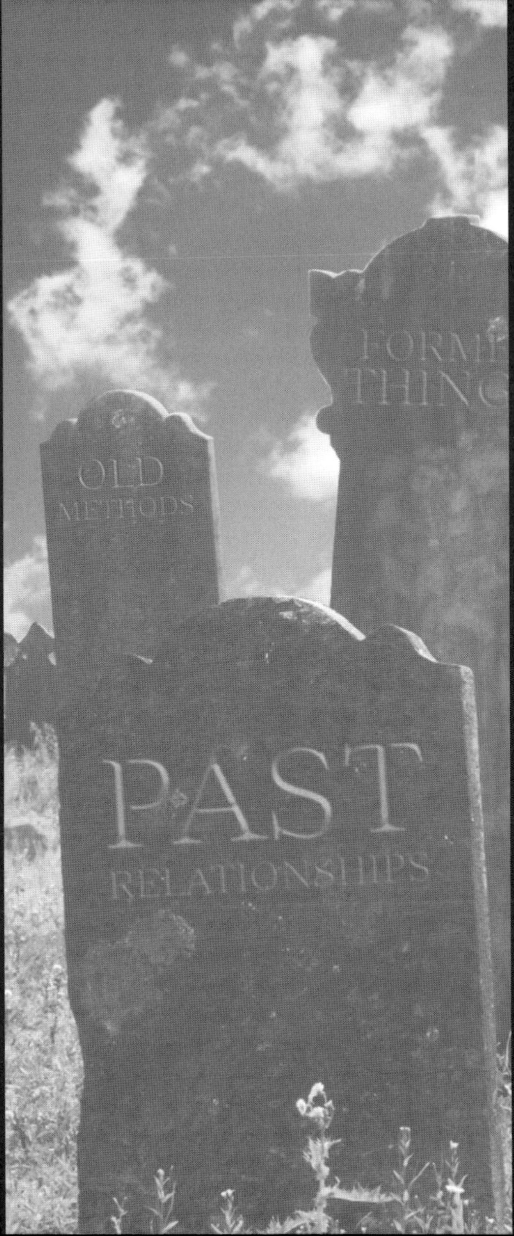

OLD
METHODS
PAST
RELATIONSHIPS

Lot's Choice

"Flee for your lives! Don't look back, and don't stop anywhere in th
plain! Flee to the mountains or you will be swept away." Genesis 19:1

Lot's life was filled with dead relationships – people who only wanted to use his 'assets' but had no respect for his opinions and dignity. It was Lot's fault though! He chose to make his home in a place seething with the smell of sin. The Angels told him to make a run for it with his wife and two daughters. Lot chose a small town called Zoar to run to before judgement arrived. The Angel declared, "But flee there quickly, because I cannot do anything until you reach it." (Genesis 19:22)

God cannot do anything with your future until you deal with the relational orbits around your life. Some people's gravitational pull is so strong on the believer that it drags them away from rooting their wills into the purposes and will of the Lord. Jesus said that, 'if your right eye causes you to sin, gouge it out and throw it away. It is better for you to lose one part of your body than for your whole body to be thrown into hell.' It all sounds pretty dramatic, yet the severity of losing out on everything eternal for the sake of one earthly desire or connection shouldn't be understated. If you're dating someone who isn't enthusing you in your walk with the

Lord, it's time to do the right thing and break it off! If you're connected to someone in business who is bent on breaking not only the rule of law but the rule of integrity, it may be time to go your separate ways! If you feel like someone is stealing your heart away from its true purposes, whether it's a longstanding friend or the luring of a new attraction with the opposite sex, it's time to abandon the connection.

God wants to move afresh in your life, yet He is often 'held up' by indecision and compromise. This is your moment to get set free into all that God has for you. While you continue to nurture your Ishmael, you delay the coming of your Isaac. Accept no substitutes for what is the perfect and pleasing will of God!

They may be nothing like the Cities of Sodom and Gomorrah, yet the principal remains the same. Many believers remain in churches that have lost their life and vitality and are hampered by a leadership that has no real desire to see souls saved, lives changed or God glorified. They've simply either made it their goal to maintain a strict moral code of behaviour or made the church a social institution with no bearing to real discipleship or walking in the Spirit. Many Christians find that in putting old connections and old friends first, they deny the very reason for which they were saved – to walk the road of faith and power in intimacy with Jesus. The very essence of faith is to be constantly moving into deeper waters and to be constantly exploring more and more of the nature and the ways of God. With so many churches located around the harbours of compromise and complacency, it may be time for you to take heed and lead by way of faith to the new things God has planned for you. It may be a little intimidating and unsettling, yet your future (and the future of many, many people) depends on it.

Mary Mary

"On the first day of the week, very early in the morning, the women took the spices they had prepared and went to the tomb. They found the stone rolled away from the tomb, but when they entered, they did not find the body of the Lord Jesus. While they were wondering about this, suddenly two men in clothes that gleamed like lightning stood beside them. In their fright the women bowed down with their faces to the ground, but the men said to them, "Why do you look for the living among the dead? He is not here; he has risen! Remember how he told you, while he was still with you in Galilee: 'The Son of Man must be delivered into the hands of sinful men, be crucified and on the third day be raised again.'"

Luke 24:1-7

Mary Magdalene, Joanna and Mary the Mother of Jesus were grieving the loss of the man upon whom they had hung their dreams, hopes and aspirations. They were on a mission to anoint the dead – to honour and respect someone who had been light in their darkness and power in their weakness. They'd forgotten His promise that in three days He would rise and forgotten the purpose for which He came. They were consumed by His death.

Many believers spend their lives in cemeteries of past moves of God, old relationships that have failed, past hurts, as well as past successes from bygone seasons. The multitudes of churches across the country not only reflect amazing past moves of the Holy Spirit but also, sadly, an inability to move out from the past into a future of newness and expansion.

It was time for Mary to leave the cemetery and declare to her world that Jesus was risen. It's our time to do the same – to leave the places where He was and join Him in the place where He now is. It's called 'the next chapter' of your destiny!

Frozen in Time

'But Lot's wife looked back, and she became a pillar of salt.'
Genesis 19:26

Looking back is never a great choice for God's people! Lot's wife represents many of us who have left the past, are on our way to a brighter future, yet secretly hanker after the things that were left behind. It begins with our emotions that are stirred by our fondness to certain memories. Our imagination kicks in and occupies itself with 'what if' scenarios. It's not long before we glance back into relationships that are no longer meant to be and reconnect ourselves with our distant past. It may be a past romance or simply a relationship that served a former season of your life but has no rhyme or reason to continue into the brand new season God has for you.

It's time to stop looking back! Three guys once wanted to follow Christ and yet each of them wasn't willing to have the courage to put Jesus first and foremost. They each looked back. One just loved his home comforts, another loved his home responsibilities and another just loved home! (Luke 9:57-62). Home is said to be where the heart is yet the Psalmist declared, "Blessed are those whose strength is in you, who have set their hearts on pilgrimage. As they pass through the valley of Baca, they make it a place of springs; the autumn rains also cover it with pools. They go from strength to strength ...' (Psalm 84:5-7). Our real home and citizenship is with God in heaven. That's why Jesus had 'no place to lay His head', or in today's lingo – 'no place to hang His hat!' When this world becomes your home you can so easily miss the exhilaration of going from strength to strength and the joy of turning deserts into springs of life and success.

Hebrews 10 verse 38 declares, 'But my righteous one will live by faith. And if he shrinks back, I will not be pleased with him.' Let's not shrink back, look back, turn back or even stand at the back. Let's run the race set before us and move into the 'next big thing' that God has in store. None of us want to be frozen in time!

and another thing...

"Then he said, 'Here I am, I have come to do your will.' He sets aside the first to establish the second." Hebrews 10:9

God set aside the broken law of Moses to establish the new and living way of Jesus. He'll do the same in your life. He'll remove all that is broken and bent, old and torn, in order to replace it with something that's both new and whole. Old rituals are replaced by fresh relationship where the Holy Spirit can take you in to the next stage of the journey that He planned for you before time began!

Dead and Buried

'Then Abraham rose from beside his dead wife and spoke to the H
tites. He said, "I am an alien and a stranger among you. Sell me som
property for a burial site here so I can bury my dead."' Genesis 23:3

The expression 'bury my dead' is used three times in this chapter in Genesis, and the expression 'bury your dead' is used a further four times. It wasn't enough for Sarah to die, she needed to be buried! She was the Mother of Promise and the faithful wife of the Father of Faith. Her season had ended and needed to be marked by a respectful burial.

Burials are an essential part of life. They effectively close a chapter and, in doing so, allow a new one to be opened! It's difficult, especially when the person has been united with you in faith and hope, desert and desolation.

In our lives there is often a lot of unfinished business where things have died in our hands or in the hands of others. They're dead, but not buried. They have no more life in them, yet we live amongst them in vain hope that they may one day spring back to life. Sometimes we're too scared to bury our past, just in case a burial takes the dream just outside of the gamut of God's powerful hand.

The truth is that both the resurrections of Lazarus and Jesus came from the place of burial. God cannot resurrect your past unless the past has not only died, but been buried and left in the vaults of true trust. Without a proper burial, many people live in a state of procrastination – always putting off what ought to be done in the hope that what they wish could happen would happen. Instead of making steps into a new chapter, they remain on a blank page that eventually leads to a state of confusion and compounded sadness.

It's when your past is both dead and buried that the next season emerges, fashioned directly by the hands of the God who knows best.

Burials belong to man, esurrections belong to God!"

Breaking up is always hard to do

'The Lord had said to Abram, "Leave your country, your people and
your father's household and go to the land I will show you."'

Genesis 12:1

Leaving is always difficult. Even leaving your fears can be fraught with fear. Yet it has to be done. Abraham, in order to inherit a promise that was reflected by the multitude of stars in the night sky, had to leave all he ever knew and loved.

There were three attachments that needed to be broken. Firstly, to leave one's country is to leave everything familiar – the smells, the way the sun falls upon the land at sunset, the wildlife and the seasons.

Secondly, to leave one's people is to leave a common language, a common understanding and a common bond. Thirdly, to leave one's extended family is to leave your source of affirmation, companionship and united history.

The Bible tells us that many years before, Abraham's dad had set out with the family from Ur of the Chaldeons towards Canaan, yet when they came to a place called Haran, 'they settled there' (Genesis 11:31). Did Terah receive the same promise as Abraham and yet fail to leave all that he had grown to love and cherish? Many people set out for their Canaan experience yet find that their relational ties are too strong to all that they hold dear.

Many people say that, 'it's better the devil you know than the devil you don't'! And that's why many stay attached to not only their comforts and conveniences but also to their fears and failures. It's better, though, to know no devil at all and to obey the promptings of the Holy Spirit!

For Abraham to enter into the beginnings of a promise that would even encompass each one of us today, he had to step out by faith into his unknown future. He had to leave past memories, past acquaintances and past loved ones. He had to move to a place he'd never been before.

It's time to lock the gates of your personal cemetery and throw away the key.

Half Way House

'By faith Abraham, when called to go to a place he would later receive as his inheritance, obeyed and went, even though he did not know where he was going.' Hebrews 11:8

The book of Hebrews defines faith as 'being sure of what we hope for and certain of what we do not see'. (Hebrews 11:1). If you can see it, it isn't faith! If you can't see it, yet obey the call to leave it all behind, it's a sign that faith is both present and active!

Haran represents a place where a majority of Christians dwell – halfway between what they want and what they really really want. They live their lives torn between two loves – a love for all that's familiar and a love for the God of their future. It becomes a City of Doubt and Double Mindedness where people do what they don't really want to do and become who they don't really want to be.

It's time, however, to break camp! It's time to hear God's promises afresh and to take heart and heed to the Spirit's promptings. There is a land that flows with both the milk of new strength and the honey of new sweetness for all who dare to pack their bags and head out in obedience and worship.

Some say that Abraham should have left his nephew Lot behind and not taken him with him into the land of promise.

Lot had not only grown up under his uncle's care, but he was also a part of Abraham's father's household. In the Hebrew language, the word 'Lot' means not only 'dark coloured' but also 'concealed'. Partial disobedience will always conceal a part of our vision until the 'veil' is removed. It wasn't until Abraham and Lot parted company that God allowed Abraham to see again both new land and the legacy of promise that He had set aside for him. (Genesis 13:14-17).

If you don't move with the cloud, you'll die in the desert.

Old Flames

'Do your best t
come to me quickly, fo
Demas, because h
loved the world, ha
deserted me and gon
to Thessalonica.'
Timothy 4:

It always amazes me that whenever we choose to walk the road less travelled to reposition ourselves into a new land of promise, an opportunity arises that directly challenges our intention to obey and depart. For some it's an old flame, for others it's an amazing job offer, and for others it's a temptation that is almost too good to be true! If that is where you find yourself today, it's a sure sign from heaven that it's time to 'fight the good fight of faith' (2 Timothy 4:7) and arise!

Accept no substitution, refuse all compromise! It's time to leave it all behind and head for the 'Isaac' of your future.

The Story of Ruth

'Naomi said to her, "Go ahead my daughter." So she went and began to glean in the fields behind the harveste As it turned out she found herse working in a fiel belonging to Boaz who was from th clan of Elimelech. Ruth 2:

Boaz became Ruth's kinsman redeemer. He also loved her and became her husband and she rose to become the great grandmother of David.

'As it turned out' is, perhaps, the most understated expression in the Word of God. Her repositioning from being a poor widow to becoming a prosperous wife was not by accident. Ruth's faithfulness to her bereft mother in law was what led her into her incredible destiny.

> *"... where you go I will go and where you stay*
> *I will stay. Your people will be my people and*
> *your God my God. Where you die I will die, and*
> *there I will be buried." (Ruth 1:16)*

Ruth made it her goal to support, strengthen and honour the mother of her dead husband. It was in the pursuit of this that she met Boaz. In a world where people are trying to push their way to the top, she learnt the secret that would be taught by Jesus many centuries later – 'the last shall be first and the first shall be last'. (Matthew 20:16)

Ruth had repositioned herself by returning to Israel and

by serving the life of another. Her reward was substantial. Joseph had a similar experience. He served the butler and the baker by interpreting their dreams while his had floundered beyond all recognition. His service was rewarded when Pharoah exalted him to become second highest in the land.

To lay down one's life for the sheep and for God's church is to lose oneself in the name of love and obedience. It's in these places of selflessness that God dwells with the fullness of His power! You are not forgotten!

"When they came back from the tomb, they told all these things to the eleven and to all the others." Luke 24:9

ey left the tomb and began to preach. It's time to leave your tomb and begin to declare esh that He is risen (and so shall you be!).

2. Broken Dreams

A time to mourn

'The Lord said to Samuel, "How long will you mourn for Saul, since I have rejected him a king over Israel? Fill your horn with oil and be on your way, I am sending you to Jesse of Bethlehem. I have chosen one of his sons to be king."' 1 Samuel 16:1

For months I mourned over the death of my first marriage. It may be a common thing in our world today yet the tearing of emotions and the heartbreak that accompanies it can be like the passing of a tsunami. No one can anticipate the turmoil that surrounds what was never 'meant' to happen. It wasn't until I read this passage did I feel like any hope would return to my inmost being.

Samuel had lost the heart of his king and he found himself grieved, demoralised and demobilised by the man he'd hung his hopes upon. God had to speak to him. His words were to do with the closing of a chapter and the opening of a new one – 'fill your horn with oil' and search out the next big thing! King David was only a shepherd boy when Samuel found him yet he became the greatest king that Israel would ever have.

Your future may right now be out on the windswept hills just waiting to be discovered! There's a new anointing upon you to no longer cleave to that which is irretrievably dead, but to search for that which is currently alive, yet totally unseen.

This is your opportunity to change your gaze from the past to the future and to be 'defrosted' by the fresh power of the Spirit of the Lord. Your future awaits!

In picking up my 'fresh horn of oil', God re-energised me to reconnect fully to seeing lives saved and people's hearts restored. He began again to bless my life. In being candid about my personal circumstances, I want you to know, however, that I fully believe in the sanctity of marriage and God's jealousy of it. In no way do I want to encourage people to leave a marriage because it's all out of love or if the partner is not walking with the Lord. The future is always worth fighting for.

There are times and circumstances, however, after much water has passed under the bridge, where letting go and moving on becomes the most necessary (yet the most painful) thing to do. It needs much thought and time as well as wisdom from Christian leaders around you.

In every loss, no matter how small or how big, there is a legitimate and important season for mourning. Without a season of grieving, many emotions lie both suppressed and un-dealt with, causing perpetual instability in future times and seasons. God didn't tell Samuel not to mourn, but to stop overstepping the 'season' for mourning! Some Christians have a 'Job' experience that lasts for forty years simply because they never put an end to their mourning! Some say that Job's 'wilderness' experience only lasted around nine months! His life was then restored to twice the blessing he'd previously experienced. 'Weeping may remain for a night' yet there is a time, a set time, when night turns to day and joy becomes the hallmark of the next and newest season. (Psalm 30:5).

Memories

'After the death of Moses the servant of the Lord, the Lord said to Joshua son of Nun, Moses' aide: "Moses my servant is dead. Now then, you and all these people, get ready to cross the Jordan River in the land I am about to give them – to the Israelites."' Joshua 1:1-2

For Joshua to rise up, Moses had to die. It wasn't just the man Moses, but the memories of Moses. The Israelites had to put behind them not just the memories of great success like the deliverance from the hands of Pharaoh and the parting of the Red Sea, but the energy-sapping memories of failure. The wanderings in the wilderness as well as the judgements from the Lord had to be put behind them before the uprising of the Joshua generation.

It may be that you too face both good and bad memories that have hampered your pursuit of the next chapter of your journey of faith. It's time to close the photo album and get ready to cross your Jordan.

The Christian faith is all about saying 'Goodbye' to the past and saying 'Hello' to the future. It sounds easy, yet it is the hardest thing in the world for so many people to do. To say 'Goodbye' is to let go of all that has become precious and all that has seeped its way into our identity and personalised our memories, our dreams and both loved ones and places. To say 'Hello' is to embrace an unseen future with the assistance of an unseen God. It's a place where faith meets fear and says 'It's time to go'. Joyce Meyer once said that 'if you're scared, do it scared'. Your future waits for your obedience to overturn your emotions. It's time for faith to arise.

It's a place of complete trust, yet from it new dreams are birthed and new horizons emerge.

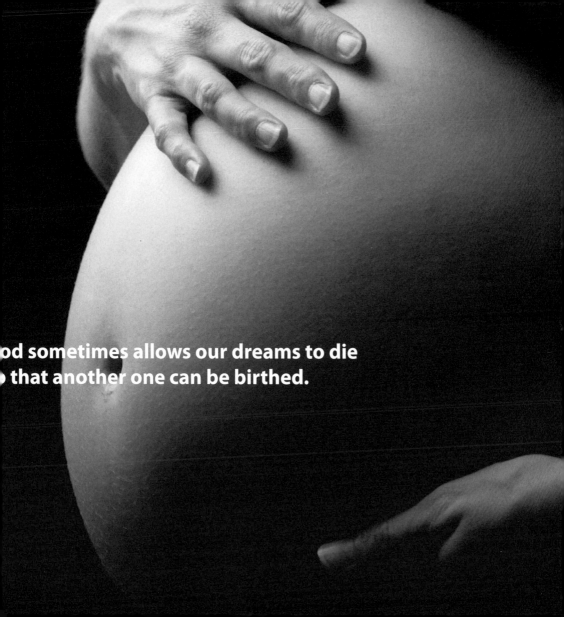

od sometimes allows our dreams to die
 that another one can be birthed.

When Experience Fails

←——————— **15 feet** ———————→

'When He had finished speaking, He said to Simon, "Put out int
deep water and let down the nets for a catch." Simon answered,
"Master, we've worked hard all night and haven't caught anything. B
because you say so, I will let down the nets." When they had don
so, they caught such a large number of fish that their nets began t
break.' Luke 5:4-6

Experience is useless when new ways are needed. For Simon, there was only fifteen feet difference between port and starboard – what difference would that make to an experienced fisherman, yet Jesus knew that it would make all of the difference! The boat, the nets and the fish all remained the same – the method was what needed to change and this is true for so many with unfulfilled dreams.

It's true that Jesus could simply have moved the fish fifteen feet! The purpose, however, isn't just to pour out miracles from heaven, but to bring us into intimacy with our Maker and Shepherd. They that know their God are the ones who are set to do mighty exploits (Daniel 11:32). Through the act of obedience, humility becomes a portal to the intimate knowledge of God that then leads to mighty exploits. In failing to humble themselves before the Lord and in sticking with old tried and tested methods, many find their nets left dangling and empty instead of full and heaving. 'We've never done it this way before' are the last words of anyone who wishes to be left dangling in the annals of history instead of caught in the crossfire of tomorrow's blessings.

No more regret

'His servants asked him, "Why are you acting like this? While the child was ill, you fasted and wept, but now that the child is dead, you get up and eat!" He answered, "While the child was still alive, I fasted and wept. I thought, 'Who knows? The Lord may be gracious to me and let the child live. But now that he is dead, why should I fast? Can I bring him back again? I will go to him, but he will not return to me." Then David comforted his wife Bathsheba and he went to her and lay with her. She gave birth to a son, and they named him Solomon.'

2 Samuel 12:21-25

We all have to learn the lesson of David. His son lay at death's door while David fasted and pleaded for God to touch him. After seven days his son died. David immediately got up, washed, ate and comforted his son's mother. Soon after that, he received a new son into the world – Solomon! His ability to move on shocked his servants, yet because he was able to move on, he went on to establish his throne through the birth of Solomon.

Whatever has not worked out in your life, whether it has been the death of someone you've loved, the collapse of a business or simply a seeming lack of blessing from the Lord, never grow bitter towards Him. David put on a new set of clothes and worshipped (2 Samuel 12:20). The Psalmist urges us to take off the garments of heaviness and put on the new garments of praise.

David surrendered himself afresh to the sovereignty of his God. He did not allow for any roots of bitterness to penetrate his heart. However confusing the outcome of your life is and however dark it may appear ... it's time to bend the knee in worship and adoration. He is God and we are not.

To give birth to a Solomon, there has to be a turning of the page in the book of life.

In verse 15, Bathsheba is called Uriah's wife. In verse 24, Bathsheba is called David's wife. Only Jesus can take you out of the cemetery of past sins and lift the shame and guilt of our misgivings and mistakes. Through destroying the works of the devil and breaking the power of sin (1 John 3:8), Jesus is able to take us out of the place of failure and condemnation. Not only did David draw a line in the sand, but so did God. David returned to a collision course with destiny. Solomon in Hebrew means 'beloved of the Lord' – all stigma broken and all past removed.

It's time by the grace of our Lord Jesus Christ to leave the cemetery of both regret and past sins and move ourselves into the next season of our lives. It's time to cease reliving, reviewing and revisiting the past in both our mind and our conversation. It's time to put an end to post mortems. It's time to take off the CSI outfit and begin to investigate our future and not our past.

There are Solomons waiting to fill up our worlds. Will you walk out of your self-imposed exile and set yourself apart for the sake of your future? It begins with worship.

God will not do everything we ask of Him. He's not a slot machine. He's not one to dictate to. What we ask of Him may or may not be the will of God. If He gave us everything we asked for, many of us would not be holding Him so closely today.

The Potter's Wheel

'So I went down to the potter's house and saw him working at the wheel. But the pot he was shaping from the clay was marred in his hands; so the potter formed it into another pot, shaping it as seemed best to him ... "like clay in the hand of the potter, so are you in my hand, O house of Israel."' Jeremiah 18:3-5

We are the clay, God is the potter! Sometimes through the bumps and bruising of life, we are misshaped and no longer line up with the Master's design. Sometimes we are used for a season and then reformed for a much bigger season ahead. In it all, God's intention is to create a vessel that's durable, expansive, as well as shaped according to His purpose and pleasure. Allow the hand of God to place you on His wheel and fashion you as seems best to Him. Allow Him to take out all that doesn't belong in the clay of who you are! Allow Him to create a vessel of honour fit for the Master's use!

It was a noble venture – the building of a new School of the Prophets! It was under the supervision of one of the greatest Old Testament prophets, Elisha. It all began with the cry 'Look, the place where we meet with you is too small for us'.

Many times in life, we begin with honourable ambitions and godly desires. It may have been a pursuit of the calling of God into full time ministry. It may have been a desire to evangelise and win truck loads of people to Jesus Christ. It may have been a desire to feed the hungry and heal the weak.

As with one of the prophets, it's easy in the midst of holy pursuits for our 'axe head' to fall into the water. To lose one's cutting edge is common, even for men and women who have been greatly used by God for world-changing endeavours. To regain one's cutting edge is far less common! The propensity to sit by 'the rivers of Babylon' and weep is one that may cause us to live out the rest of our lives in hurt and regret, despising anyone who looks both fresh faced and bushy tailed! To get your edge back requires three things.

Firstly, an awareness of where you lost it; secondly, a throwing of a piece of wood at the place of falling, and thirdly a reaching out to retrieve it!

Sometimes we lose our edge when someone turns against us and we allow bitterness to spread as roots within our souls. Sometimes it's because the lure of the world becomes too great and we find ourselves distracted by the love of money or the love of pleasure. Sometimes we simply lose it through weariness and exhaustion.

To understand when we lost our cutting edge is to know what has caused our bluntness and ultimately what to repent of. The throwing of wood is the application of the cross that both forgives us of our sins and restores back to us all we've lost and all that's been taken away. The reaching out is the application of our faith that not only receives a fresh anointing but dares to step out again in the purposes for which God has set us apart!

As the iron began to float in the water, the man reached out to take it. Why live any more in the bluntness of the past when the sharpness of destiny awaits? There are axe heads floating by God's power in the streams below you. Go on – take it and get back to the job at hand – building God a house so that the earth shall see that our God reigns!

3. Past Methods

The Good Old Day

'In the third year of Hoshe
son of Elah, king of Israe
Hezekiah son of Ahaz kir
of Judah began to reign
He removed the high place
smashed the sacred stands ar
cut down the Asherah pole
He broke into pieces the bronz
snake Moses had made, for u
to that time the Israelites ha
been burning incense to
(It was called Nehushtan.
2 Kings 18:1-

Hezekiah was twenty one years of age when he became king. He represented a new generation of leadership. He took away the worship of both foreign gods and the worship of old methods! God once used the bronze serpent as a vehicle to heal multitudes of people simply by looking at it. They'd gone on to keep it for over 500 years and even had a favourite name for it! Nostalgia can become the Christians greatest enemy. When sentimentality is lifted above spirituality, the church always moves off the cutting edge and into ineffectiveness. Every church and every Christian has memories, but they can never be immortalised.

Ecclesiastes 7 verse 10 says, 'Do not say, "Why were the old days better than these?" For it is not wise to ask such questions.' Memories always have a tendency to romanticise the good times and numb the not so good times of the past. Often things weren't nearly as good as you have imagined them! Why were the old days better? They weren't – only different! It's time to stop romanticising, philosophising and sentimentalising. It'll keep you safe from the ever present fatal danger of being stuck in the past.

It's the same for His church. God wants you to be a part of a vibrant and flourishing church. Yet the way God creates it is through journeying the church through lean and sensitive seasons. Every co-worker in Christ has to understand that their church can't be sparkly all of the time. There are deserts to cross and rivers to navigate, yet through it all, God's presence is upon it. It's at times like this that God doesn't want you to so much count His blessings, but worship the God of all blessing, showing Him your utmost love for Him by following every movement of His cloud and His fire. Obedience in the desert will mean a flourishing in the future.

Not long ago, I was driving up the Rhonda Valley in Wales and noticed all of the Presbyterian churches, Methodist churches and Pentecostal churches that had now been turned into bingo halls and carpet warehouses! I know that we all need carpets, but this was ridiculous! Each of these buildings heaved with people in the early part of the twentieth century. Now each has either closed or collapsed to become a remnant of its former self! I felt the Spirit of God speak to me and say, "Ray, you're looking at a bunch of fossils". A fossil is the skeleton of something that used to have life, yet no longer does. He went on to say to me, "They didn't know how to negotiate the seasons of destiny". Methods are never holy – only biblical truth and wisdom. This is why the church throughout the ages has missed out on so much from the vaults of heaven. People have mistaken methods for holiness. It's time for us to be diligent in negotiating our own pathways out from the past and into God's brand new future.

Methods are not holy - Biblical principles are!

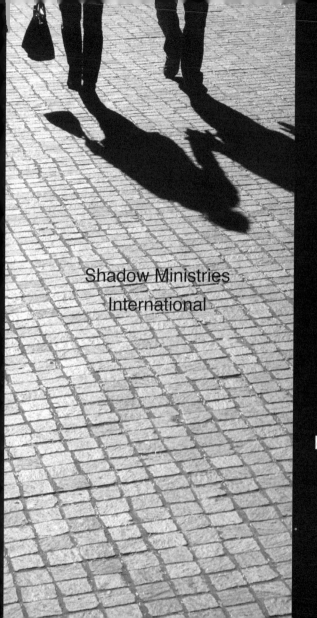

Franchising Opportunities

Shadow Ministries
International

'As a result, people brought the sick into the streets and laid them on beds and mats so that at least Peter's shadow might fall on some of them as he passed by.' Acts 5:15

God does not clone His methods. If He had, Peter would have started 'Shadow Ministries International'. Moses would have started 'Rod Ministries Incorporated'. David would have franchaised his 'Sling Ministries' and Samson would have done well with 'Jawbone Ministries'. If you look closely at a number of television ministries, you can see that method cloning is a vital part of some people's ministry platform! Everything from Miracle Springwater to Miracle Numbers can be found. It may look exciting, yet the real effect of these ministries is to lead people away from reliance upon the Holy Spirit and onto a reliance on 'holy' methods and ways. It's often said that these things are simply a point of contact that releases faith in God, yet many are in actual fact a replacement for real faith in God. It's good that Paul never started 'Handkerchief Ministries International' and Jesus never coined the phrase 'Spit Power – it's good for you!' It's time that we only use methods that are up to date with this current part of the journey that Jesus is leading us on. When those methods are in danger of becoming our 'Nehushtan', God quickly moves us on to a new place that requires new wisdom and new ways.

Another's Anointing

'Then Saul dressed David in his own tunic. He put a coat of ar mour on him and a bronze helmet on his head ... "I cannot go in thes he said to Saul, "because I am not used to them." So he took them o Then he took his staff in his hand ...' 1 Samuel 17:38-40

Are you wearing Saul's armour? Are you trying to be someone that you're not called to be? Are you fighting battles that you're not called to fight? Are you using earthly armour to fight spiritual fights? It's time to resist the spirit of imitation and take off the armour that was designed for another person at another time and place. You have an anointing that needs both to be released from within you and put on over you. It's your original flow of power that comes by an original relationship with God. Why did Saul offer his armour? Was it to humiliate David? Was it driven by jealousy and insecurity? For whatever reason, the devil wants to dress you in another person's 'anointing', using old ways for new battles. There's a sling nearby and it's time to pick it up!

The only unchanging thing is God and His word. For everything else, there's change.

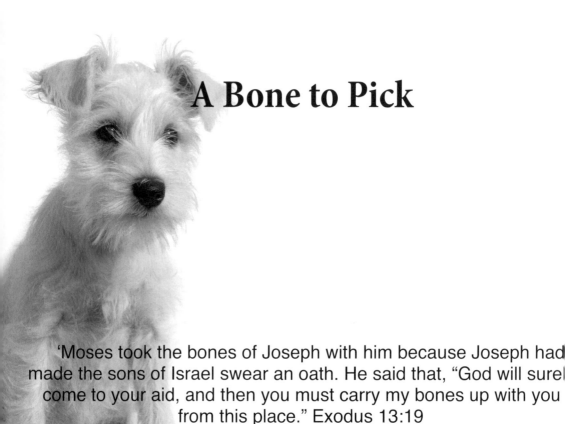

A Bone to Pick

'Moses took the bones of Joseph with him because Joseph had made the sons of Israel swear an oath. He said that, "God will surely come to your aid, and then you must carry my bones up with you from this place." Exodus 13:19

Even though the writer of Hebrews credits Joseph's desire to have his final resting place in the land of Canaan as a mark of his great faith, it's essential that we don't force the next generation to carry our dead bones of tradition with them upon their journey of faith. They need the presence of God, not the bones of past ways. There is often a fine line to be taken between honour that's due to people who have paved the way before us and a worship of their ways and practices.

Moses, carrying the dead bones, took the Israelites out of Egypt and into the wilderness. It was Joshua, carrying the Ark of the Covenant that took them out of the wilderness and into the land of Canaan. The bones were still amongst them but they were the bones of respect, not the bones of tradition and worship.

I have met so many Christians who, like Moses, carry close to their hearts the bones of past moves of God and past memories of His power. They're always reminiscing! Their favourite expression is 'I remember when'. Don't get me wrong – we thank God for everything and for everyone that's gone before us but I can't help thinking that they've replaced the Ark of His Presence with the bones of the past.

Every time a church grows and advances forward, the bones of Joseph seem to arise from the most unexpected places. The 'Elder Brother Syndrome' that liked things as they were before the Prodigal returned lies hidden in the depths of our humanity. People remember the time when worship was more intimate, you knew most of the people present and the Pastor at least said 'hello' to you before they left the service. They remember when they played guitar and when their best friend shared anecdotes around the communion table. They used to love it when the preacher would wink at them as he made reference to the joke that they shared together around the impromptu lunch after bumping into each other at their local gym!

The challenge for every growing person and every growing church is to make sure that the Ark of His Presence always precedes the bones of respect. The presence of God carries with it His love that values you not for your achievements but for your very existence. It carries His celebration of all that you've been and all that you're becoming. It carries His call to be transformed into His likeness and it carries His desire for intimacy and trust through the required seasons of change and adaptation.

If you hanker after 'the former things', you'll find yourself surrounded by dead bones of past champions and pioneers. If you desire to move into 'the next big thing', you'll need to surround yourself with the Ark of His Presence and Power. It's a choice we all have to make and it's a choice worth making.

Much prayer coupled with an unwillingness to change equals the Spirit of Religion.

The Gentle Whisper

'At this she turned around and saw Jesus standing there, but she did not realise that it was Jesus.' John 20:14

It wasn't until Jesus called out her name 'Mary' that she recognised that it was her Saviour and her Lord. He obviously had a new look! She thought He was the gardener. The men on the Emmaus road thought Him to be a fellow traveller and some of the disciples thought Him to be a ghost! His voice remained the same but His 'look' had changed. Upon recognition, Jesus urged Mary not to cling to Him but to go to the disciples and tell them about what had happened. Jesus could have returned with the brightness of the Mount Transfiguration experience but instead He returned only recognisable by a flicker of revelation. Why? He was preparing the way for the Holy Spirit and didn't want to overstate His presence. He was about to go to heaven and send the full power of heaven in the form of the third person of the Holy Trinity.

No one was ready for this new and fresh manifestation of Jesus – and it's the same today.

For Elijah, God was not in the earthquake or the fire or the powerful wind that tore the mountains apart. He was in the gentle whisper! While many wait for explosions from heaven as a sign of the presence of God, they can easily miss His presence because of its uncharacteristic softness and quietness. Not every new season is like the last!

I've seen some 20 year olds with the heart of an 80 year old ... and I've seen some 80 year olds with the heart of a 20 year old. Youth is not an age, it's an attitude.

Traditions always seem to feed off the law. We admire Eric Liddle for his famous stand at the 1924 Olympics by refusing to race on the Sabbath. He stuck by his convictions despite the cost. How many others, though, have done the same and actually missed out on a piece of destiny and history for the sake of empty traditions and superceded laws?

tradition

4. Old Seasons

The Winter is Over

'My lover spoke and said to me,
"Arise, my darling,
my beautiful one, and come with me.
See! The winter is past;
the rains are over and gone.
Flowers appear on the earth;
the season of singing has come,
the cooing of the doves
is heard in our land.
The fig tree forms its early fruit'
the blossoming vines spread their fragrance.
Arise, come, my darling;
my beautiful one, come with me."'

Song of Songs 2:10-13

The winter is over! When the blustery winds and cold fronts have forced us to baton down our hatches and retreat to our inner worlds, it can easily become a place from where we never depart. Disappointment, hurts, pain and loss can cause us to miniaturise our worlds, never venturing far from our shelter.

Just as when the winter turns to spring and people can be seen still wearing their thick winter coats, we need to be reminded by God that as He ushers in a new season in our lives, we need to arise, put aside our fears, leave our failures and misgivings, and start to prepare ourselves for the new things that God has prepared. The early fruit is forming but only those who rise up out of their tears and grief will see and possess.

Give thanks in all seasons,
for this is God's will for you in Christ Jesus.
(1 Thessalonians 5:18 paraphrased)

The Gardener

'My mother's sons were angry with me and made me take
care of the vineyards; my own vineyard I have neglected.'
Song of Songs 1:6

"We had joy, we had fun, we had seasons in the sun, but the hills that we climbed were just seasons out of time."

Terry Jacks' 1973

Terry Jacks big one hit wonder from the 1970s, that was also covered more recently by Westlife, hit a nerve in the hearts of many people. Each of us have had brilliant seasons of hill climbing, beach combing and leaf kicking but to make it all last forever is to attempt the impossible. Our times of joy and fun simply become seasons out of time! To be like the children of Issachar who understood the times and seasons (1 Chronicles 12:32) is to gain a huge advantage in successfully navigating the seasons of life.

When a season is coming to an end it's generally accompanied by certain manifestations! Things that were once 'easy' become a little difficult, things that once shone now look a little jaded, and things that were once fruitful now bear little fruit. All of these manifestations can indicate the closing of one chapter and the coming of a new one.

Out of all of the four seasons in a year, autumn is often seen as the most beautiful, yet the trees are emptying themselves of their now dead leaves and it appears that nature is taking a backward step. Gold brown is actually the look that leaves get when they're past their sell by date!

> Jesus said this about the change of seasons in our lives – "I'm the true vine, and my Father is the gardener. He cut off every branch in me that bears no fruit, while every branch that does bear fruit he prunes so that it will be even more fruitful." (John 15:1-2)

A gardener will prune back a rose bush but only to get it ready for a new season of growth. It's the same with you. When God is about to take you into a new season of growth and expansion, friendships falter, finances deplete, anointing dissipates and difficulties arise. Instead of your life looking like it should, full of prosperity and blessing, it looks a little on the skinny side! Instead of a bush, you're left with a stick!

It's important in life to never compare last season with this season, someone else's season with your season and the end of a season with the middle of a season. You can't compare a bush with a stick, or a harvest with a paddock full of seed. In actual fact, a brown field without seed looks identical to a brown field with seed. The only one who knows the difference is the farmer! It may appear like your life is a brown field scorched by the sun and wind, yet it's actually a field that's been seeded by the 'gardener' ready for the autumn rains and coming fruitfulness!

To embrace any new season you have to be prepared to look ugly for a short while. While many believers hang on to all of their leaves and live in past seasons and blessings, it's courage and vision that allows you to let go of all that is yesterday and set yourself apart for all that is to come.

Many times church leaders try to hold onto every person in their congregation in order to present themselves as leaders of a growing and vibrant group of Christians. Nobody likes a 'negative revival' yet it is often the case that some people have to be let go of or, better still, sent off in order to set the stage for future growth. It's often the case when a church begins a building fund and launches into what will become a place of expansion. As the heart of commitment (especially financial) rises, a number of people often use it as their opportunity to leave! It may not be right but it happens. For some, however, it's actually the work of the 'gardener' cutting off every branch that fails to bear fruit. To let go and trust God is the best thing for the leader to do. Knowing that God is doing some trimming and some pruning in order that His church might be more fruitful than ever before is heartening! He's getting you ready for a fresh move of the Holy Spirit. Because He never stops moving, even the slight depletion is a move of His Spirit – a very secretive one! To everyone looking on who hasn't yet received the wisdom of the Men of Issachar, it looks like you're failing and haven't got what it takes. Nothing could be further from the truth!

Give thanks to God in all seasons until He comes up with the next part of the plan!

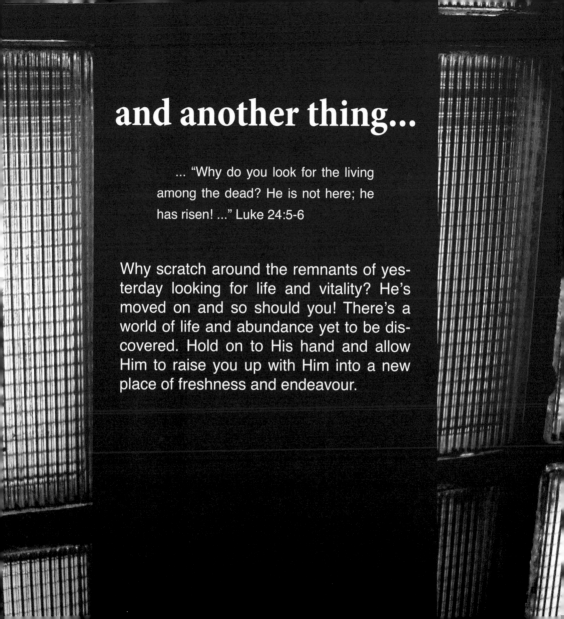

and another thing...

... "Why do you look for the living among the dead? He is not here; he has risen! ..." Luke 24:5-6

Why scratch around the remnants of yesterday looking for life and vitality? He's moved on and so should you! There's a world of life and abundance yet to be discovered. Hold on to His hand and allow Him to raise you up with Him into a new place of freshness and endeavour.

MOSES IS
DEAD!

'After the death of Moses the servant of the Lord, The Lord sa
to Joshua son of Nun, Moses' aide, "Moses my servant is dead..."
Joshua 1:1-2

Every 'man of God' is accompanied by a set of ordained leaders, methods, songs and traditions. Every new 'move of God' is accompanied by a new set of ordained leaders, methods, songs and traditions. Problems arise when we sanctify methods, canonise traditions and immortalise people used of God!

What worked for one season may not necessarily be the best for the coming season. Smith Wigglesworth was brilliant in his time, but there'd certainly be more than a few eyebrows raised if he was ministering today. At the funeral, many wondered 'What are we going to do now?', such was the weight of influence this one man carried! The overwhelming truth though is that God raises up different people for different generations. In calling certain people 'great men of God' instead of 'men of a great God' we often run the risk of over egging the pudding with reliance upon great men instead of upon a great God.

Sometimes it's good and right to declare that Evan Roberts of the great Welsh revival is actually dead! Sometimes it's a healthy thing to declare that Charles Finney of the Great American Awakening is dead as well as Moses, Joshua, David, Ezra, Daniel, Peter, James and John and your great uncle Daryl. They're dead but you're not! This is your season to rise and be the man or woman of God you're called to be. This is your opportunity to stand in the gap and bridge the revelation divide between Jesus and humanity.

The successful fulfilment of destiny is having the wisdom to know how to negotiate the seasons of life.

The unfolding of your destiny is seasonal. He remains the same, but what He does changes.

Mastering Reinvention

'No one sews a patch of unshrunk cloth on an old garment, for the patch will p[ull?]
away from the garment, making it tear worse. Neither do men pour new wine in[to?]
old wineskins. If they do, the skin will burst, the wine will run out and the wine w[ill?]
be ruined. No, they pour new wine into new wineskins, and both are preserved[.]
Matthew 9:16-17

Before God can do a new thing, He has to create a new vehicle for the new thing to travel in! The old vehicle served its purpose well to take us from A to B. It will not suffice to take us from B to C. One of the hardest things to ever do in life is to reinvent! It takes courage to change habits, style, friends and pathways that have become a part of the very fabric of our lives. Most people reinvent out of necessity. Their vehicle of destiny lies broken and burnt out on the road of destiny and they're left waiting around for a new vehicle to arrive!

The best time to reinvent, however, is before what you're currently travelling in comes to a halt. Every season has a beginning, middle and an end! It has a period of acceleration, exhilaration and anticipation that is then followed by a period of increasing frustration and exhaustion. It's at this time that the next season needs to be perceived, recognised and ushered in. In that way, you never lose momentum and never find yourself in a stop-start world. You move from a gentle slowing down to a refreshing increase in pace. It takes smart leadership of one's life and church to anticipate the need for change before there's even a need for change!

Motion sickness

'When Jesus saw him lying there and learned that he had been in this condition for a long time, he asked him, "Do you want to get well?"' John 5

The man lived in a state of suspended animation. No longer living on the edge of the pool, he would never be the one to receive healing through the stirring of the water. His life was caught between a distant dream and a world of borrowing and begging. When Jesus turned up he went straight for the jugular – "Do you really want to be made well?"

Maybe you find yourself merely going through the motion of religion and ritual? Maybe you've lost your drive to walk into victory and conquest? Sometimes we find ourselves caught in another time and place. We've lost our focus and allowed our passion to die. Our destiny is on pause while we feebly search for answers in all the wrong places. It's about time you stopped looking for the living amongst the dead, leave the pools and cemeteries of your lives behind, and receive His power to walk into the next season of our lives. If God wants to resurrect past dreams, display your trust in His ability to do so by letting go ... completely ... and absolutely! To hold on is often the very thing that prevents both the opening of brand new horizons as well as the resurrection of old one!

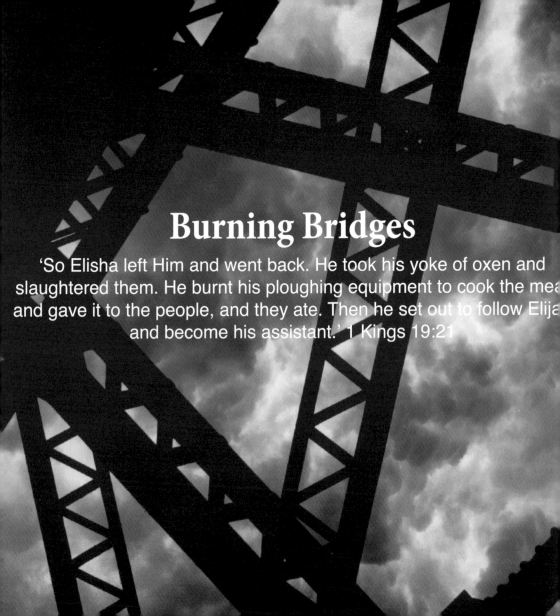

Burning Bridges

'So Elisha left Him and went back. He took his yoke of oxen and slaughtered them. He burnt his ploughing equipment to cook the mea and gave it to the people, and they ate. Then he set out to follow Elij and become his assistant.' 1 Kings 19:21

For Elisha to eventually receive a 'double portion' of the spirit that was on Elijah he had to burn all of his bridges to the past. He had to go past the point of no return. Joshua once declared, "Consecrate yourselves, for tomorrow the Lord will do amazing things among you" (Joshua 3:5). A setting apart of oneself to the worship of God always precedes a pouring out of God's power. When Jesus said to His potential disciples 'come follow me and I will make you fishers of men' (Matthew 4:19), they immediately left their nets and followed Him. Consecration precedes consummation by the power of the Spirit.

There is no doubt that God has planned amazing things for your life. All He needs is for you to leave your 'nets' and set yourself apart for God. No ifs, no buts.

The older we get, the harder it is to embrace the changing seasons in one's life.

He goes before you!

'By day the Lord went ahead of ther
in a pillar of cloud to guide them on thei
way and by night in a pillar of fire to giv
them light, so that they could travel by da
or night.' Exodus 13:2

When the pillar of cloud moved, the Israelites moved. When it stopped, they stopped. If they didn't move with the cloud, they would have been left unprotected from the burning heat of the day. If they didn't move with the fire, they would have been left open to the bitter cold of the desert night. The manna went where the cloud went. The heat and the protection went where the cloud went. It's the same with you! God's Spirit doesn't stay in the same place and time – He's on a journey and wants to take you on His journey to the Canaan of His promises fulfilled. When you follow the cloud, it doesn't matter where He takes you, even in the barren wilderness, God will look after you. If you've been open to His leadings and 'obeyed and went', you may be wondering 'why am I in the place I'm in?' The overwhelming answer to that question is because He is there! Whether it's desert wastelands or well watered fields, God is with you and you are with Him. In fact, in the first few chapters of Ephesians the expression 'in Christ' is repeated a staggering ten times. To be in Christ is to be inside Christ – inside His covenant of protection, provision, power and promise. He isn't just in you but you're in Him!

5. Past Hurts

Jabez's Joy

'Jabez was more honourable than his brothers. His mother had nam
him Jabez, saying, "I gave birth to him in pain." Jabez cried out to t
God of Israel, "Oh, that you would bless me and enlarge my territo
Let your hand be with me, and keep me from harm so that I will be f
from pain." And God granted his request.' 2 Chronicles 4:9-10

Jabez got his name from the pain inflicted upon his mother at the time of his birth. The Bible gives no indication as to whether the pain was physical or emotional. She may have been abandoned and abused at the moment of Jabez's arrival into the world. Whatever the circumstances, Jabez was lumped with not only a name (which actually means 'pain') but also with an orientation towards painful experiences. He was born in pain and lived in pain, yet was determined not to continue in pain. Jabez tapped into the scarlet thread of faith that runs through the entire length of the Word of God – including His direct ancestry of Jacob, Isaac and Abraham!

One of the classic songs of this current generation is the song by the Australian Natalie Imbruglia called 'Torn'.

The chorus states:-
> *I'm all out of faith*
> *This is how I feel*
> *I'm cold and I am shamed*
> *Lying naked on the floor*
> *Illusion never changed*
> *Into something real*

I'm wide awake
and I can see the perfect sky is torn
You're a little late

I'm already torn!

This song reflects the Jabez spirit that hovers like a low lying cloud over a generation of people who feel like life has turned on them and there's no way out from the rips and tears of life. Jabez, however, rose up and believed that his God was a restoring God. He believed four things.

Firstly, he believed that God would bless him! His cry was heard from heaven because it lined up with the will of God! The Psalmist declared boldly in Psalm 23 verse 6,

'Surely goodness and love will follow me all the days of my life ...'

His plan for you right now is to give you 'a future and a hope'.

Secondly, he believed that God would enlarge his territory! Most fences and boundaries are found on the side of gullies and at the base of cliffs. It's the same with us – both the gullies of fear and the cliffs of impossibility shout at us that we can go no further!

Psalm 16 verse 5 and 6 tell us a different story –

> 'Lord, you have assigned me my portion and my cup, you have made my lot secure. The boundary lines have fallen for me in pleasant places; surely I have a delightful inheritance.'

The will of God for your life is never defined by the boundaries of fear or past failure. It's defined by His destiny! Jabez had an inkling that his inheritance was much larger than the spirit that'd he'd inherited.

Thirdly, he believed that God's hand would be with him! They say that there is only one thing worse than being hated, and that is being forgotten. At least when people hate you, they're thinking about you! Being forgotten, lost or abandoned is a feeling that invades many people's souls and lingers throughout their lives. Jabez, however, believed that God had not forgotten Him and believed that the thoughts and touch of heaven was all he needed to rise beyond his circumstances.

Psalm 139 verse 7 says

> 'When can I go from your Spirit. Where can I
> flee from your presence.'

Jacob woke up and declared 'Surely the Lord is in this place, and I was not aware of it.' (Genesis 28:16). It's time for us to arise from our sleep and believe that God's hand is upon us and His Will will rule and reign!

Fourthly, Jabez believed that God would free him from pain! Psalm 103 verses 2 and 3 declares

> 'Praise the Lord, O my soul, and forget not all
> of his benefits who forgives all your sins and
> heals all your diseases.'

Isaiah declared that 'by his wounds we are healed' (Isaiah 53:5).

God is ready to heal all of us from not only the tearings of sin but also from the inner pain of rejection, inferiority and loss. Jabez believed that and 'God granted his request'.

The story of Jabez is one of the shortest found in the Bible, yet one of the most profound. It's about a man who refused to live in the cemetery of his mother's making. It's about a man who failed to accept that defeat and failure were going to accompany him into his future. It's about a man who realised that it was his time to leave the cemetery and head for the Canaan of the covenant of God.

May the same conviction and belief rise in your heart today as the God of Jabez became, by faith, your God and your Lord.

"Weeping may remain for a night but rejoicing comes in the morning."
Psalm 30:5

"...you turned my wailing into dancing; you removed my sack cloth and clothed me with joy."
Psalm 30:11

Tale of
Two Son

"Forget the former things
do not dwell on the pas
See I am doing a new
thing! Now it springs up
do you not perceive it?
am making a way in th
desert and streams in th
wasteland
Isaiah 43:18 -1

Joseph, in the land of his suffering, gave birth to two boys. The firstborn was called Manasseh which is derived from the Hebrew word for 'forget' and the second was named Ephraim, derived from the Hebrew word for 'twice fruitful'. To give birth to an Ephraim you must first give birth to a Manasseh. Joseph declared at Manasseh's birth that, 'God made me forget all my troubles and all my father's household' (Genesis 41:51). His troubles were great. Abused, abandoned, rejected, mistreated, incarcerated and the greatest of all – forgotten. Yet, God helped him to no longer dwell on the past. Upon Ephraim's birth, he declared 'It is because God made me fruitful in the land of my suffering' (Genesis 41:52). That is what God is an expert at doing – creating fountains in wastelands and rivers in deserts. He gave Isaac a hundredfold blessing after he sowed his seed in a time of famine (Genesis 26:12) and He'll do the same for you.

It all begins when we forget all that has been before and cast our inner eyes of faith onto all that lies before us. God is doing a new thing, but it needs us to perceive it. Will you?

He Restores my Soul

"If a man steals an ox or
sheep and slaughters it
sells it, he must pay ba
five head of cattle for t
ox and four sheep for t
sheep." Exodus 22

When God restores, He gives back more than that which was ever taken away. When the Psalmist declared in Psalm 23, 'He restores my soul' it was this that he had in mind. Sometimes our soul gets torn apart by the loss of things that we love as well as by our adversary whose sole purpose is to steal, kill and destroy. For whatever reason things have gone missing, departed or simply been taken away from our lives, God is our restorer. He gives back more than that which was ever taken away from us in the first place.

The oldest book of the Bible is the book of Job. It's a powerful illustration of God being a restorer. The story begins with all that Job possesses being taken away from him with his wife encouraging him to 'curse God and die'. The story ends with Job receiving twice as much as all that was taken away. Two passages stand out in the 'in-between' time in Jobs' life. Firstly he declared, 'though he slay me yet will I hope in Him...' (Job 13:15). He removed all of the small print and sidebars that so often get in the way of our relationship with God. He took away old deals, agendas and provisos and simply declared his surrender to the love of God.

Secondly, he declared, 'I know that my Redeemer lives, and that in the end He will stand upon the earth' (Job 19:25). He had a revelation that God was his Redeemer and that he would again see Him face to face, despite the current difficulties.

It's this revelation of the nature of his God as redeemer and restorer, as well as his empty handedness that positioned him for the outpouring that he was about to receive.

God's will is always to 'restore the years that the locusts have eaten' (Joel 2:25 KJV) and to give back to you 'pressed down, shaken together and running all over' (Luke 6:32 KJV).

It's time to empty your hands of all other agendas and worship your Redeemer and your Restorer until you too can declare in faith that you know for certain that your Redeemer lives!

and another thing...

'This is what the Lord says – your Redeemer, who formed you in the womb ... who says of Jerusalem, 'It shall be inhabited,' of the towns of Judah, 'They shall be built,' and of their ruins, 'I will restore them,' who says in the watery deep, 'Be dry, and I will dry up your streams.' (Isaiah 44:24-27)

Your God leaves no place untouched by the mighty power of His redemptive hand! He rebuilds our lives from the inside out and transforms us into something that has never been seen before – by others or by ourselves.

To redeem is to buy back. The cross of Jesus bought you back into the Hands of God. Surrender everything to Him and He'll do everything for you according to His will and His Word.

52
DAYS

"So the wall was completed on the twenty fifth of Elul, in fifty two days. Wh
our enemies heard about this, all the surrounding nations were afraid and lo
self-confidence, because they realised that this work had been done with th

When God restores, He puts back together stronger and faster than that which was originally destroyed!

'Bigger, better, brighter' is the catchphrase of the restoring God. The walls of Jerusalem had laid desolate for over seventy years, yet their restoration only took fifty two days! As the hand of the Lord was with Nehemiah, so His hand is with you. Although you may have been plundered by the work of your adversary throughout your childhood or teenage years, God is ready to place His strength and power on the place of your weakness and loss.

> *"My grace is sufficient for you, For my power*
> *is made perfect in weakness."*
> *(2 Corinthians 12:9)*

Paul declared, 'for when I am weak, then I am strong'. God builds Cities of Strength upon the fault lines of human weakness.

He is the same God today as He always has been. He will continue to show His strength to all who call upon Him in humility and faith.

Restoring Fortunes

"I will repay you for the years the locusts have eaten – the great locusts and the young locust, the other locusts and the locust swarm my great army that I sent among you." Joel 2:25

In a sovereign sense, God allows things to take place that are certainly not his desired will or plan. When someone becomes a follower of Christ and His Spirit lies within them, the only power that the devil wields is through the power of our negligence, not through the power of his wishes and desires. God is your protector and God is your strong tower. God, therefore, has the ability to repay you for each year that the great locust spent on his rampage of destruction. The King James version of the Bible uses the word 'restore' for 'repay'. He can restore your confidence, dignity, emotions, imagination, sanity and inner health. He can fill you with love, joy, peace, patience, kindness, goodness, faithfulness, gentleness and self control.

> 'For you did not receive a spirit that makes you a slave again to fear, but you received the Spirit of sonship. And by Him we cry, "Abba, Father".' (Romans 8:15)

Being a child of God means that every spiritual blessing is now yours. Allow God to restore His fortunes into your life for every year that they were absent!

'The glory of this present house will be greater than the glory of the former house,' says the Lord Almighty. 'And in this place I will grant peace', declares the Lord God Almighty.'
(Haggai 2:9)

When God restores, He gives back much more than what was taken away. The promise is for you, your family and your future. You shall go from glory to glory and from faith to faith!